HOCKEY...
under winter skies

P. Shostak

HOCKEY...
under winter skies

Paintings and Text
by
Peter Shostak

YALENKA ENTERPRISES INC.

Yalenka Enterprises Inc.
5001 Georgia Park Terrace
Victoria, BC   V8Y 2B8
Canada

Canadian Cataloguing in Publication Data
Shostak, Peter, 1943 -
Hockey—under winter skies

ISBN 0-9691180-5-8

1. Hockey in art. 2. Shostak, Peter, 1943—Childhood and youth.
I. Title.
ND 249.S5A2 2000   759.11   C00-910486-0

Design by Peter Shostak
Photography by Vince Klassen
Layout by Desktop Publishing Ltd.

Printed and bound in Canada by Friesens

For my wife, Geraldine, who has unselfishly supported my artistic career by providing intelligent encouragement, much-needed criticism of my paintings, and invaluable editorial comment on my writing. Without her complete dedication to the required secretarial and office support, my ability to continue working in the studio would have been greatly diminished.

INTRODUCTION

I am asking those who remember:

Dick, Jane, Sally, Tim and Puff; lard pail lunch buckets, school inspectors;

felt boots, moccasins, rubber boots;

Rosebuds, Lucky Elephant and Cracker Jack popcorn, puffed wheat squares;

Gene Autry, The Lone Ranger, Ma and Pa Kettle, Francis - the talking mule;

card games: King Pedro, cribbage, canasta;

outdoor games: Anti-I-Over, Seven-Up, Kick the Can, Jacks, Splits, Scrub, Prisoner's Base, Drop the Hankie, Hopscotch, Fox and Geese, Five Hundred, Pom Pom Pull Away, Crack the Whip, and

HOCKEY … *under winter skies*;

to share with the young people in your lives what it was like to grow up forty or more years ago.

Getting a ride home (close-up)

Hockey is a game born in a land of young people desperately needing something to do; in a land where ponds, sloughs, streams, rivers and lakes—millions of them, are frozen for five months of the year. Playing hockey made winter almost bearable.

Yes, I played hockey. We all played hockey. It did not matter if you were big or small, fat or skinny, young or old, had new skates, old skates or no skates. Everyone played hockey.

We did not play inside a building where the ice was smooth and always clear of snow. Our ice patch had twigs and grass, ripples and bumps, cracks and gouges. We played outside on a patch of ice on a nearby pond, or on a flooded area in the school or farm yard.

We did not play inside where there was no wind and where the bright lights were always on. During the day, we played by the light of the low winter sun. When it slid behind the distant horizon, we played in the dark by the light of the stars and the moon. Sometimes, we even played by the light from a truck or car. On our farmyard rink, the moon was eventually replaced by a bright yard light which we could control with a switch.

We did not play inside on a rink where the ice surface was surrounded by boards and remained the same size for the entire season. The perimeter of our rink was first formed with pieces of firewood laid end to end and then by a ridge of shoveled snow. Each successive snowfall pushed in the sides of our rink so that, by springtime, our playing surface was quite small.

We did not play inside on a rink with blue lines, centre lines, face-off circles, referees, whistles, scoreboards, player boxes, penalty boxes, or goal creases. Our goal posts were boots or pieces of wood. The distance between the two posts was determined by whether your team was winning or losing.

The boys won't have to walk home

My preschool world consisted of my family and our farm animals.

Our family of seven included my mother and father and four younger brothers. We lived in a humble three-room farmhouse surrounded by an assortment of farm buildings. Both sets of grandparents, many uncles, aunts, and cousins all lived within two miles of our farm.

In September of the year I turned six, I left this small, secure farm world to go to school. I was now grown up.

My two-room country school was only a half mile from our farm and had fifty students in grades one to nine. On the first day of school, I hesitantly and shyly entered the junior classroom. There was a row of desks for each of the five grades and from my desk in the Grade One row, I was introduced to a bigger world. I soon learned to sit still, to speak English, to do arithmetic and, most importantly, to read and write.

However, it was outside the classroom where I really learned how to be part of that expanded, more complex world. As a first grader, I managed to stay out of the way of the older students. To minimize physical pain, I quickly learned where I belonged and what I should and should not do. The trick of surviving until Grade Two was knowing what I could get away with in Grade One.

Typically, our schoolyard was run by the oldest and, naturally, the biggest boys. Here, I was taught how to play Anti-I-Over, Hopscotch, Seven-Up, Drop the Hankie, Five Hundred, Scrub, marbles, jacks, tag, cricket and hockey.

Maybe someday we will get to play on a real hockey rink

My introduction to hockey began, sometime after Halloween, when the ground was frozen hard and the first snow had fallen. The schoolyard leaders enlisted the help of most students in packing down the soft snow in a rectangular area, which was to be that year's hockey rink.

Everyone was expected to help. Even if you were only six years old, had no idea of what was happening, did not own a hockey stick, and had never seen the game played, you joined in. All of this semi-coordinated flurry of activity was exciting.

I did not immediately know the purpose of this curious follow-the-leader tramping of snow. The youngest students were always the last to know. I did not ask for, nor did I expect, a detailed explanation.

Like tears, on a cold windy day, sliding down the contours of your face and finally arriving at your chin, schoolyard knowledge trickled down from those who knew and were in charge. For me, that tear of knowledge reached my chin when a Grade Two student looked at me in disgust and said, "We are making a hockey rink - stupid."

"What is a hockey rink?" - I wanted to ask, but did not. There was little of the normal fooling around. Making a hockey rink was very serious business.

Stones and sticks were removed. A perimeter of round unsplit firewood, laid end to end, formed a boundary around the soon-to-be ice surface. With the snow tramped down and the wood neatly arranged, it was time for phase two - flooding. This task was performed by the older boys who carried pail after pail of water from the well. The water was poured onto the packed snow, turning it to slush, which was leveled out before it was left to freeze. That first flooding of the soon-to-be playing surface took countless pails of water.

Today we started making a hockey rink

Those involved in creating the ice surface relied upon the cold of winter days for assistance. When the temperature was well below freezing, the water, combined with the packed snow, froze very quickly. As the layer of ice built up and became smoother, each spilled container of water covered a larger area.

No formal announcement was made for all to know that the hockey rink was ready. It was time to play when the pails were replaced by hockey sticks. The few players, who could afford to purchase sticks from the general store, had their new stick blades neatly wrapped with a layer of black tape. Those who had old battered sticks, survivors of the previous winter of games, also wrapped their broken, cracked blades with a layer of tape. Homemade sticks were fashioned from a discarded hockey stick handle and a piece of plywood. The two parts were held together with tin from a metal can and plenty of small nails. These players tried to disguise the homemade look with a double layer of tape.

Still others had to be content with hockey sticks cut from appropriately bent saskatoon or willow saplings - no tape required.

Time to play hockey

Like the boys carrying water in pails from the well to the rink, I daily carried information, about school and all that was new to me, home to my brothers. They would have the advantage of knowing something about the school and the schoolyard. Soon they, too, would be all grown up.

Life was never the same after I brought the game of hockey home. Before we were able to flood a playing rink in our barnyard, before we could keep a small patch of ice on a frozen slough clear of snow, before we had real hockey sticks, a puck and skates, we played kitchen hockey.

With school rulers or small pieces of apple box boards for hockey sticks, a checker or a marble for a puck, and the kitchen floor as the ice rink, we learned to play hockey. Our kitchen was a perfect place to play. It was warm, the two-mantle kerosene lamp hissed as it provided a bright white light and the sheet linoleum on the floor was an excellent substitute for an ice surface. One goal was the doorway between the kitchen and the dual purpose living room/bedroom. The other goal was the doorway, at the opposite end of the room, leading to the entry porch, where all of our boots, shoes and outdoor clothes were kept.

Nightly, the kitchen floor was polished with our knees.

Where do you think the boys are?

From the radio broadcasts by Foster Hewitt of Hockey Night in Canada, we learned to be, not only kitchen floor hockey players, but also commentators.

"And the puck bounces off the kitchen chair and is picked up by Billy. He shoots, he SCORES…!"

"The score is now 38 to 32."

"No, it isn't - it's only 37."

"It's 38!"

"Goal doesn't count! You raised the puck more than six inches."

"No, I didn't!"

"Yes, you did… doesn't count, score is still 37, 32."

These games almost always ended when our parents could no longer stand our exuberant play, accompanying disputes and play by play commentary. Sweaty and tired, we reluctantly put away our hockey sticks and puck until the next evening.

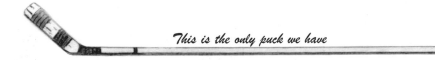

This is the only puck we have

In Grade One, after spending many recesses as a spectator, I grew confident in knowing that I too could play hockey. I noticed that occasionally the puck would pop out from between the many legs and sticks and glide to a vacant corner. Like a cat patiently stalking a mouse, I could be in a corner waiting. For a brief second or two the puck would be all mine and since neither team recognized my potential as a hockey player, I could shoot it in whichever direction I pleased. Now all I needed was a stick.

Armed with an axe and an idea of what a stick should look like, it was time for me to go shopping in the willow bushes for my first hockey stick. After sizing up what must have been a hundred or more potential sticks, I managed to cut one free from the snow and frozen ground.

Back in the warmth of the farmhouse kitchen, I carefully peeled the bark and trimmed both ends to the correct length. Yes, my hockey stick was heavy, and maybe it could have had a more pronounced bend for the blade, but it was just what I needed to claim a corner of the hockey rink.

In Grade Three, using a discarded hockey stick handle and a piece of plywood for the blade, I made my first, almost real-looking, stick. The biggest challenge was securely attaching the blade to the handle. I had observed the homemade efforts of the older boys and concluded that a piece of tin from the lid of a sardine can, shaped around the heel of the stick and blade and nailed through with thin blue shingle nails, was probably the best solution. A layer of carefully applied black hockey tape strengthened this crucial joint and gave the stick a store-bought look.

This should make a good hockey stick

My first homemade hockey stick had a much shorter life span than the time it took to make it. My arrival at the schoolyard rink, proudly displaying my carpentry skills neatly wrapped with black tape, did not go unnoticed. The stick became a target for one of the bigger players who delighted at the first opportunity to give it a whack. I spent the rest of the game holding back tears and hoping that my damaged stick would somehow heal or, at least, stay in one piece until the teacher rang the school bell.

That winter, many improved models of my homemade hockey stick accompanied me to the hockey rink and I was finally regularly selected to play for one of the teams.

Our version of the hockey player draft took place either daily or just on Mondays. Daily selections were necessary if the pool of players available to play on any given day greatly varied from the previous day. This was especially so during flu season or whenever some other illness kept students home from school.

Two oldest and probably best players served as captains for the hockey season. The ritual of team selection began when one of the captains tossed a hockey stick to the other captain. A one-handed catch of the tossed stick was followed by the captains, in turn, moving their grasp, hand over hand, up the handle until the top was reached. The captain, who was able to get the last firm grip and successfully swing the stick once around the upper part of his body, got first pick from the group of patiently waiting players. Depending on how much of the handle was left to grip, that last hold could be just a two or three finger one.

If the stick was dropped during this last crucial maneuver, first pick went to the other captain. When you were selected was an indicator of how much you were valued by the other players. It was an indication of your worth.

Noon hour hockey draft

My first skates were double-bladed bob skates that had to be strapped to my boots. They were a great disappointment. They were useless. The person who invented them probably never had the misfortune of watching a youngster try and skate on them.

Since I found these pieces of aluminum impossible to skate on, I quickly discarded them and remained without skates until Grade Six. Actually, most of the students who played on our school rink had no skates.

Shortly after my sixth year of schooling began, our two-room school was abruptly closed. In the name of progress, we now had to endure a bumpy, dusty, smelly, hour and a half ride on an overcrowded bus to a new school. Here, the number of students in my Grade Six class equaled the total population of all nine grades in my former school.

It was like starting Grade One again. Overnight, my secure and comfortable school world, consisting of classmates who lived not more than two miles away from our family farm, expanded to include students living as far as thirty-five miles from each other.

Next year we will make a bigger rink

SHOSTAK '92

Our new school had a regulation-sized outdoor rink with boards and lights. The pressure of not having skates became unbearable. My father finally agreed to buy me a pair. I could hardly endure that bus ride home on the Monday when I was to get proper skates. Soon I, too, would be gracefully gliding on the ice in pursuit of the puck.

Was I in for a surprise! First, the skates Dad bought were not new. Not only were they not new, they did not have back guards. But, at least they were real skates and they fit. My biggest disappointment was yet to come.

When I first stepped unsteadily on to the ice surface, my tentative movements had no resemblance to those of the skaters at my new school. I was more awkward than a cow walking on ice. There was something very wrong with these skates. That is why the previous owner traded them in for a better pair. I was convinced I needed the support of the missing back guards to keep the edge of my skate blades firmly in contact with the ice. Instead, my skates splayed out and it looked like I had two broken ankles.

Nevertheless, I persevered. With each outing on our pond, my opinion of the skates slowly changed. Using a hockey stick for support and wearing an extra pair of socks in my skates with the laces pulled as tightly as possible for snugness, I was able to propel myself across the ice surface.

I could hardly wait to play hockey. All I needed to do was to learn how to stop and shoot the puck without falling down, to turn, to skate backwards… Not to worry… One skill at a time.

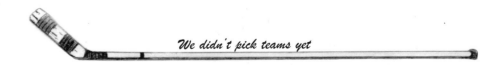

We didn't pick teams yet

When I did not have skates and played hockey in my tall, thick, protective, felt boots and rubbers, there was no real need for additional shin protection. However, when I graduated to playing on skates, it became very evident that winter long johns and pants provided little protection from the pain inflicted by a hard puck and sticks.

A layer of three or more comic books, held in place under each pant leg by red rubber jar rings, saved my shins until I was given a pair of real shin pads.

Pucks, bought at the local store, came in two sizes. A smaller variety of the regulation-sized puck best suited our skills and physical strength. Invariably, our one and only puck got lost in the snow and did not reappear until the spring thaw, three or more months later.

It's not that cold

Like cutting slices from a stick of salami, we cut pucks from long, round pieces of wood. A cutting team of three was most efficient. One person sat on the long piece of wood in the cradle and the other two pushed and pulled at either end of the crosscut saw. As the blade moved back and forth across the wood, we chanted "ours", "theirs", "ours", "theirs", "ours". We guessed on which push or pull a new puck would be cut free and fall on the snow to join the growing pile of pucks.

Our farm horses also provided a good supply of frozen, almost round road pucks. With such a plentiful supply, we were not too disheartened when our real puck was buried in the snow.

I did most of my hockey playing on small flooded surfaces in our farmyard, at our country school, or on larger slough rinks. Skating on a "real hockey rink" was a very rare treat.

Since adults played a minor role in our childhood hockey games, the location, size and condition of these rinks was our responsibility. Being the eldest child meant that the responsibility of flooding and maintaining a playable farmyard ice surface was mine.

Let's cut twenty-five pucks

There were distinct advantages to having our own barnyard rink. It was possible to lace up in the comfort of the house, go out and play, come back in to warm up and, maybe, have something special to eat.

We relied on Mom's creativity in the kitchen for our treats. The treats, which she preferred to make on her own without any of our help or interference, included puffed wheat squares, cinnamon buns, and baked pyrohy filled with either cottage cheese, sauerkraut or prunes.

And then there were the treats, such as cookies, doughnuts and apple pies, which we enjoyed helping her make. Mom always made extra dough so that we could make our own small pies. Metal lids from jam or peanut butter jars served as our pie plates. We carefully rolled out the small balls of pastry and placed them in the lids. Apples were thinly sliced and sprinkled with cinnamon and sugar. A layer of rolled-out pastry dough was placed on top. Our miniature apple pies were complete when the upper and lower crusts were trimmed and the edges were neatly pressed together with a fork. Last of all, before proudly placing our creation into the hot oven, two or three holes were cut in the upper crust to permit steam to escape. Our apple pies tasted so good.

We liked to help Mom make pyrohy, especially if she let us have some of the leftover dough. These small lumps were rolled out flat and then fried on the hot wood stove. If we wanted the dough to cook evenly and not bulge out with air pockets, we made holes in the flat dough with the tip of a knife. Armed with forks, we surrounded the kitchen stove and patiently monitored the cooking of our treats. Once the dough was lightly browned on both sides, we sprinkled cinnamon and sugar or spread butter over the hot fried dough.

Still playing for the street championship

The proximity of our ice rink to the house also made it easier to motivate my younger siblings to join in, even if only for a short period of time. When the weather was ideal, this small ice surface was the place you hurried to. Chores were completed in record time and meals were quickly eaten.

The main disadvantage of having our own farmyard rink was all of the work required to create it. Like the rink at school, this involved carrying countless pails of water to flood a suitable surface. Since the farm well was our only source of water, there was always the concern that the well might run dry. Each year the size of our farmyard rink depended not only on our ambition but also on the water supply.

Some years, after a prolonged dry summer and fall, there just was not enough water. Water for our personal use and for the farm animals was more important than water for a hockey rink. We had to be content with a playing surface of packed snow.

On Saturday Dad is taking us to town to play hockey

A hockey rink on a slough was usually larger in size. Here, we did not have to carry pails and pails of water to create an ice surface. All we needed to do was keep the ice clear of snow.

On our farm, the nearest slough was quite a distance from our warm house. Maintaining a clean ice surface and going out to play involved some hardships. It meant you could not put your skates on in the house, nor could you easily run back in to warm up. On colder days, it took some creative persuasion to convince my younger brothers to leave the warm house and accompany me to clean the rink and play hockey.

Our rink did not have any lights. During the short winter days, play after school was almost impossible. We played in the evening only when it was not too cold and the full, or almost full moon and bright stars provided the necessary light.

Maybe someone will come and give us a ride home

The rinks of late fall and early winter were the largest. As long as we did not have a heavy snowfall, we were able to keep the large ice surface relatively clear. A prolonged, heavy snowfall meant we had to spend many hours trying to clear the ice so that we could resume our hockey playing.

We tried to reduce the magnitude of the task before us by dividing the playing surface into sections. Four players meant each player had to clear only a quarter of the ice surface.

With a light aluminum grain shovel or a plywood scraper, we attacked the snow on our respective section of the farmyard rink. Before chores, between chores, and after chores, shovelful after shovelful of snow was carried to the edge of the playing surface and the ice was slowly freed from beneath the unwelcome blanket of snow.

However, as the season dragged on, and the snow continued to fall, the perimeter of the rink was diminished by the constantly growing size of the shoveled snowbanks.

During the spring thaw, nature provided us with gifts of skating areas which were as smooth as glass. This happened when winter returned with one last cold blast and froze all the spring ponds. These ice surfaces were great for skating on but not for playing hockey as there were no boundaries of snow to stop the puck from gliding and gliding and …

When is Peter going to clean his quarter off?

Living on a farm meant daily chores had to be done. Evening chores consisted of bringing water and firewood to the farmhouse, carrying water to the chicken coop, collecting eggs, making sure the water tank was full and the fire in the water tank heater was burning to keep the water warm for the farm animals, cleaning the barn, providing fresh bedding and hay for the cattle, feeding the pigs, and finally, feeding our cats and dogs. There were no holidays from winter chores.

On Saturdays, there were the added farmyard tasks of cleaning the chicken coop, bringing a week's supply of bedding straw and hay to the barn, grinding grain to make feed for the pigs and cutting down and hauling next year's supply of firewood.

Everyone was expected to help out and I did what I was physically capable of doing.

On most Saturdays, any hockey playing was delayed until all chores and extra tasks were attended to. Games involving players from several farms, when you played until you were totally exhausted and famished, almost always occurred on a Sunday afternoon.

Who is going to help unload the straw?

During my youth, Mom's taxi did not exist. In fact, getting to and from the slough, where the community rink was located, was a major effort. Most often, we had to walk. If we were lucky, we hitched a ride with someone in a cutter. If we were really lucky, we got a ride in a truck or car.

One journey to a hockey game, which remains vivid in my mind, occurred on a warm, early spring Sunday afternoon when a number of students from our school went to play a team from a neighbouring school.

The game was to be played on a rink that the host team had cleared near the dam on Moose Creek. Someone gave us a ride to the bridge on the creek, and although we could see by the tracks in the snow that others had driven vehicles on the creek bed, we were dropped off to walk the last two miles. We had not walked very far when some of the players from the opposing team came roaring down the creek bed in a car. They stopped, and since there was no room inside the car, we were invited to climb on the trunk. Somehow, all five of us with our sticks, skates and shin pads managed to drape ourselves on the slippery trunk and, as the car sped down the windy creek bed, we hung on as best we could. On which curve would we all tumble off? Fortunately, we managed to hang on and play one of those marathon games when, in the end, we did not know who had won. Our play was earnest and intense, but we were always considerate of each other. Definitely, there was no attempt at injury. We delighted in just playing and scoring. Winning was not the most important part of playing.

Getting a ride home

During my preschool years, our rural roads were very difficult to travel on. The ten mile trip to town with horses and sleigh or wagon, depending on the season, was a gruelling, all-day event. For children, this journey was an infrequent happening and occurred only during the warm summer months when the weather and road conditions were at their best.

However, with each passing year, more and more work was done to improve the roads and before long, most farmers bought tractors and trucks. Cars, vehicles which were useful only for transporting people, were still a novelty and a luxury. Dad bought our first farm truck when I was in Grade One but did not purchase our first family car until I was in Grade Six.

Even if most farmers owned a truck, there still were times during the year when the roads were impassable and we were unable to travel beyond the farmyard. In the winter, this occurred after a heavy snowfall or a blizzard.

Because it would take a week or two before most of the drifted roads were plowed open by the municipal snowplow, farmers cooperated with one another in attempting to open a narrow trail. They did this by building an "A" - shaped snowplow from several large timbers. These timbers, weighed down with a box of rocks placed on top of the frame, were pulled along the snow-clogged roads by one of the larger farm tractors. After much effort, the farmers usually succeeded in pushing aside enough of the snow to provide a passable trail.

The best road conditions were in early winter when the ground was frozen and there was not much snow. Under these circumstances, it was possible to drive a truck or car through a field and on to the frozen ice surface of the slough. The headlights of the vehicles parked next to the rink enabled us to continue our hockey games long after the short winter afternoon had drawn to a rapid end.

We could play as long as the car lights stayed on

At many of our hockey games we had two uninvited players, Farm Dog and Jack Frost. The very visible, never-tiring player, Farm Dog, delighted in just chasing the puck. In the process, he tripped and interfered with the play of those who were at the centre of the action.

The invisible player, Jack Frost, was also there to make our play less enjoyable. Unlike Farm Dog, who only got in the way of the players who were handling the puck, Jack Frost affected all players, especially those who were less active.

At first, his painful, stinging bites were felt on exposed parts of the ears, nose and cheeks. These initial attacks were fought off by pulling flaps, ear covers, or earmuffs snugly over the entire ear. A mitt could temporarily cover the cheeks and nose. Jack Frost's assault on fingers and toes was more difficult to deal with. While continuing to play, the first and only line of defence was to clench fingers into a fist inside your mitt and wiggle toes in your snowboots or skates.

The dog never gets tired of playing

Jack Frost won when white spots appeared on normally red cheeks, ear lobes or the end of noses. He won when play was halted so that we could attend to the freezing parts. Frost bite could not be ignored. He won when cold fingers and toes became stiff and wooden. Firmly holding the hockey stick became impossible. Many games were prematurely halted because there just was no escape from this cruel, invisible, ever-present player. No amount of toe wiggling, arm swinging, or jumping up and down could drive him away.

Our stiff and numb fingers and toes came back to life when someone made a bonfire and we gathered around to warm up. Under the canopy of a dark ultramarine blue sky sprayed with millions of stars, our bonfire's veil of smoke somehow seemed to connect us to the heavens.

We will go home when the fire dies down

Walking to the rink to play hockey was easier than walking home. As we played, the distance between the rink and our farmyard grew. By the time the fire died down and we began the long walk home, our warm farmhouse had moved. It was now at least twice as far away as it had been before play began.

Don't let the sparks fall on you

On a clear, cold night the steady rhythm of walking home, one short footstep after the other, was interrupted when the northern lights came out to dance for us. We never ceased to be overcome by the beauty of these dancing lights against the dark blue curtain.

When there were no northern lights to entertain us, we sought relief and distraction from our walk by talking. In words, we replayed highlights of our just completed hockey game. We talked to distant farmyard dogs. We also talked to the coyotes. Actually, we joined them in their serenade of the night heavens by sending imitation coyote yelps and howls into the cold, still night. I do not really know if the invisible coyotes were affected by our vocalizations. We liked to think that they stopped their serenade to respond to our calls.

Forgetting fatigue, hunger, thirst, aches and pains, we talked ourselves home until the next time.

The lights are dancing over our farmyard

Yes, our hockey games were played with sparse or poor equipment. We played without uniforms, without adult supervision, without any refereeing. We played on patches of bumpy, cracked ice surfaces or packed snow, without any markings, goal creases, surrounding boards or lights. We played without regard for too many rules or a time clock. We were the architects of our games. We played because we wanted to play. We were all winners.

Our games were of no importance to anyone else. There were no spectators or parents to cheer you on. The only non-participants present were the players who were too tired to continue playing. The games we played had no effect on anyone else. We did not know that it should or could be otherwise.

That was the hockey we played more than four decades ago.

On Sunday we could play all afternoon

Other titles by Peter Shostak:

When Nights Were Long
Saturday Came But Once a Week
For Our Children
Prairie Born (Illustrator)

For information about these publications, original art,
serigraphs and limited edition reproductions, contact:

Yalenka Enterprises Inc.
(Agent for Peter Shostak)
5001 Georgia Park Terrace
Victoria, BC V8Y 2B8
Tel. / Fax (250) 658-8785
e-mail yalenka@home.com
www.members.home.net/yalenka

Cover painting: *The boys will be getting new hockey sticks for Christmas*